Switching Tracks for a New Uttar Pradesh

Published in association with
Observer Research Foundation
New Delhi

ORF is an endeavour to aid and influence formulation of policies for building a strong and prosperous India. The expectations of the global community from India are immense as the country is poised to play a leading role in the knowledge age. The Foundation believes that in the next 25 years India will be one of the world's great economic powers and contribute to a significant transformation in the quality of life of humanity.

ORF complements official initiatives by exploring policy alternatives. It provides informed and valuable inputs for decision-makers in the government, civil society and business leadership of India. ORF's expertise and resources are dedicated to nation building and international cooperation. ORF pursues its goals through in-depth research and stimulating discussion.

Observer Research Foundation seeks the active cooperation from those who share this vision in a spirit of genuine partnership. Building partnerships for a global India is our motto.

Switching Tracks for a New Uttar Pradesh

Strategies Revisited

SAURABH JOHRI

ACADEMIC FOUNDATION
NEW DELHI

www.academicfoundation.com

First published in 2012
by

ACADEMIC FOUNDATION
4772-73 / 23 Bharat Ram Road, (23 Ansari Road),
Darya Ganj, New Delhi - 110 002 (India).
Phones : 23245001 / 02 / 03 / 04.
Fax : +91-11-23245005.
E-mail : books@academicfoundation.com
www.academicfoundation.com

in association with the
Observer Research Foundation, New Delhi

Cataloging in Publication Data--DK
Courtesy: D.K. Agencies (P) Ltd. <docinfo@dkagencies.com>

Johri, Saurabh.
Switching Tracks for a New Uttar Pradesh: Strategies Revisited / Saurabh Johri.
p. cm.
ISBN 13: 9788171889211
ISBN 10: 8171889212

1. Infrastructure (Economics)--India--Uttar Pradesh. 2. Uttar Pradesh (India)--Economic policy. 3. Uttar Pradesh (India)--Social policy. 4. Uttar Pradesh (India)--Politics and government--21st century. I. Title.

DDC 320.9542 23

Typeset by Italics India, New Delhi.
Printed and bound in India.

Contents

Foreword

Uttar Pradesh is by far the largest state in India and is considered the political heartland of the country. For about two decades it has been experiencing a decline in its rate of economic and social growth. Inter-state comparisons show that Uttar Pradesh is now in the bottom quartile in respect of parameters of economic or social development. Moreover, during this period the quality of governance in the state has been considerably eroded leading to rise in insecurity, poor functioning of the bureaucracy and civil services and decline in the quality of delivery systems.

By a happy coincidence the government that takes office after the Assembly elections early next year will be coterminous with the Twelfth Five Year Plan starting in April 2012, which is now in the process of finalisation. In that context, it would be timely and appropriate to examine the issues that the new government would need to focus on. While admitting that generally not much useful purpose is served by delving too deeply into the past to try and allocate credit or blame for the happenings of the period gone by, it has to be recognised that governance and growth are continuous processes in the life of a state. In that sense it is important, while drawing up a roadmap for the future, to take stock of things as they stand now and also to examine the trends over the last few years to identify areas that need strengthening, faults that need correction and directions that need change.

Against this background, the Observer Research Foundation (ORF) decided to play a catalytic role in order to debate and to recommend some priorities that the incoming government would need to focus on so that Uttar Pradesh could get the necessary push for providing good governance and move along faster on the road to development.

This study is the product of a study sponsored by ORF. It has benefitted immensely from inputs provided by a number of persons familiar with different aspects of governance in Uttar Pradesh. It incorporates the views expressed at a roundtable discussion with senior former bureaucrats and police officers, politicians, academicians, representatives of international organisations and journalists intimately familiar with the state.

The study is meant to:

(i) serve as a guiding document to reach a level of good governance less influenced by political vendettas and more by constitutional mandates,

(ii) help in prioritising issues while implementing the Twelfth Five Year Plan,

(iii) be a ready reckoner for some interesting models in the reform process,

(iv) be an agenda setter for political and social debates and

(v) help develop governance scorecards to capture the performance of the state.

It is not meant to be a commentary on any government or bureaucracy of the past, or a research document or a statistical scrutiny of the state. It is by no means an exhaustive list of recommendations but is meant to be just an indicative list of suggestions.

It is our sincere belief at the Observer Research Foundation that the recommendations contained in this paper would lead to significant improvement in governance in Uttar Pradesh and propel the state towards economic and social betterment.

— Surendra Singh,

(Former Cabinet Secretary, Govt. of India)
Honorary Advisor, ORF

Acknowledgements

A study on Uttar Pradesh, outlining models of governance and development for future growth, becomes more challenging than an analysis of the past. It needs individuals like Mr Surendra Singh, Former Cabinet Secretary of India, and a former UP cadre IAS officer, to guide such initiatives. I extend my sincere gratitude to Mr Singh to proactively initiate this study under the umbrella of Observer Research Foundation. Mr Singh continuously guided me to prioritise and be selective in sectors than be exhaustive and write about everything in the state.

Mr Sunjoy Joshi, Director of ORF, extended his unconditional support and motivated me to pursue this study. His kind gesture to extend ORF infrastructure and services was very generous. I would personally like to acknowledge and thank him for his patronage.

In addition, I also extend my gratitude to Dr Satish Misra, Senior Fellow at ORF, who has long years of experience in journalism, especially on issues of UP; he provided me with deep insights on the socio-political setup in the state and also provided all the literature support needed for the study.

I am also very grateful to Dr Ajit Kumar Singh, Director, Giri Institute of Development Studies, who has deep understanding of the development issues in Uttar Pradesh and has authored many research papers for the state. Dr Singh very kindly shared his valuable insights with us.

Undoubtedly, without the team at ORF, this effort could not have been completed. I would like to thank the researchers Rakesh Kumar Sinha, Neetika Khurana, the editor Ms Anshu John and the administrative and IT staff at the Foundation.

I would like to acknowledge the contributions of Mr Shishir Gupta at Mckinsey & Co., with whom I held many brainstorming sessions and who worked with me in giving shape to the urbanisation section of the study.

I would like to thank the participants of the brainstorming session held at ORF; all of them gave valuable inputs about Uttar Pradesh and helped me structure the report better. I was happy to see a very productive and proactive debate around the subject and hope that the present study would generate more interest amongst the active policymakers in the state and elsewhere.

Finally, I am grateful to my family who let me work during odd hours and weekends to complete the book; and without their active support this work would not have been possible.

1 Envisioning a New Uttar Pradesh

Nearly 20 crore people of Uttar Pradesh aspire to make it as the most prosperous and peaceful state in the country. There would be a significant number of people outside the state who also dream to make their home-state revive its glory.

Often compared with Brazil in population or Kenya in GDP per person, Uttar Pradesh has always figured in the bottom quartile in most of the economic and social indicators of our own country. The poor indicators clubbed with poor governance and complacent administration has further dampened the spirits to achieve larger goals. Further, the increasing rich-poor divide, politico-bureaucratic nexus and inequitable distribution of wealth has made the state a cause of concern for a number of people.

In recent years, the state is exhibiting some robust numbers around growth and other socioeconomic indicators; however the development is largely skewed with significant parts of the population still a distant away from the benefits of the numeric achievements. There is inequity in distribution of most of the provisioning like infrastructure, social services with strong cartels often sabotaging the development agenda. In addition, the quality of the provision and services are also questionable with no real measure to assess the quality.

The situation is arising primarily because the focus of development has shifted from the people to more on upward management or pleasing the masters. There is a race to show numeric achievements without any concern of whether it is affecting the lives of the common person or not. Settling personal vendettas, whether in politics or administration, has become the order of the day. There are strong bureaucratic lobbies aligned to different political parties leading to complete neglect of the preferences, priorities and perspective of the common person.

Today, the choice for people is not on who will deliver the highest growth rates, or plan lofty goals for the state but who will create an environment of trust amongst people, who will create simple and scalable models of development which will affect the everyday life and who will create a sense of safety, security and justice in the common person by honestly reforming archaic institutions.

This study largely formulates a new vision for Uttar Pradesh, and also illustrates simple doable models of reforms in governance as well as some of the key sectors relevant to the common person.

Elements of the New Vision

Every individual executes his/her choice to elect a government with primarily three elements core to his/her needs. Needs like:

1. *Economic security*: Neat and transparent systems of record of their land and other asset ownership; convenience of trade; opportunities and ease of employment; availability and access to financial services like credit, investment and insurance.

2. *Infrastructure support*: Availability of convenient transport services and road connectivity even in remote areas; ample water both for drinking as well as irrigation; availability of electricity; and safe and secure housing, and

3. *Social welfare and social security net*: Quality and relevant education for children; easy and efficient health services; social security in the form of pension, insurance, disability and medicare.

If these choices and aspirations are at the centre of state policy planning, the administration and politics would automatically align to deliver larger goals towards welfare that would further create a ripple effect down the lower rungs of administration and politics. Further, it may also encourage more democratic decision-making at all levels and empower the systems to become more transparent.

Figure 1.1

The above vision clubbed with some actionable changes in governance foundations and sector priorities could be a good starting point to draw out the reform agenda for Uttar Pradesh.

Without doubt, there are multiple sectors, themes and areas, which need reform. However a few sectors and governance levers are undisputedly the core of prosperity and peace in any state. Focus on the key sectors like agriculture, trade, finance, power, roads, housing, education and health care would automatically lead to alignment of other sectors. Similarly a strong governance foundation around safety and security, efficient officials and departments, and speedy justice would definitely improve autonomy, accountability and credibility of the government.

In the following pages, we would touch upon different aspects of governance and political reforms and discuss some of the burning issues around them and exemplify potential actionable points. The suggestions are illustrative and indicative but in no way comprehensive.

Figure 1.2

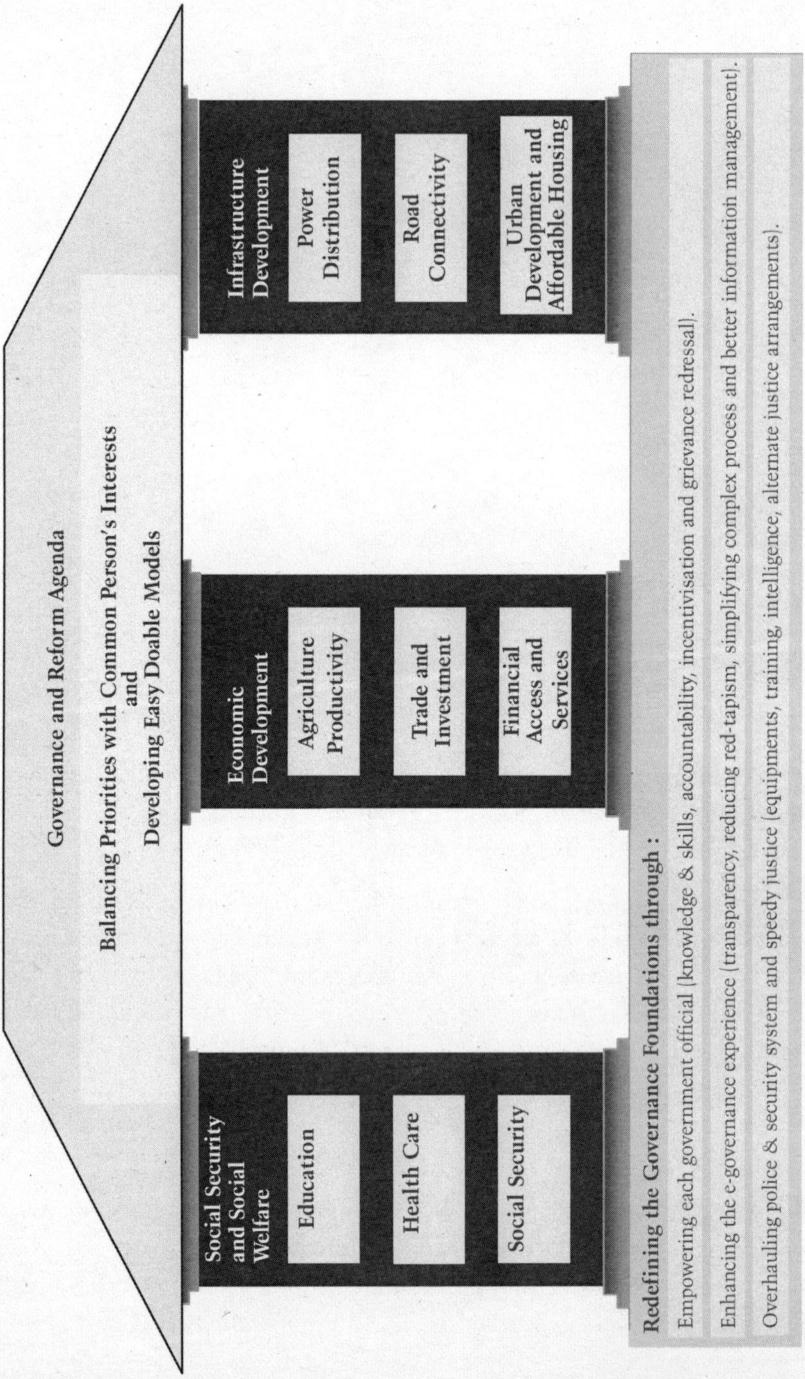
Governance and Reform Agenda
Balancing Priorities with Common Person's Interests
and
Developing Easy Doable Models
Social Security and Social Welfare
Education
Health Care
Social Security
Economic Development
Agriculture Productivity
Trade and Investment
Financial Access and Services
Infrastructure Development
Power Distribution
Road Connectivity
Urban Development and Affordable Housing
Redefining the Governance Foundations through :
Empowering each government official (knowledge & skills, accountability, incentivisation and grievance redressal).
Enhancing the e-governance experience (transparency, reducing red-tapism, simplifying complex process and better information management).
Overhauling police & security system and speedy justice (equipments, training, intelligence, alternate justice arrangements).

We would then touch upon the different sectors key to people's agenda and direct to a development journey. The key aspirations in the journey would be to achieve and sustain robust growth across sectors and balance it with improvement in social indicators like poverty, HDI etc. Since mere targets often bias the system towards only numeric achievements, we would also illustrate on ways to measure parameters like commitment from leadership, political non-interference, collective decision-making, lowered corruption, people's satisfaction levels and so on.

2. Empowerment of the government officials by developing a sound knowledge and skills base, by defining clear accountability mechanisms and methods of incentivisation and by establishing effective structures of grievance redressal within the system.
3. Unleashing the power of IT and using it to streamline complex processes, organise information and data, and making the system more transparent.
4. Overhauling the police system and ensuring speedy justice through radical reforms in police and design mechanisms to help the judiciary in achieving speedy justice.
5. Judiciary reforms, though not entirely mandated by the state government, is an important lever for change.

Measuring Success beyond Numeric Targets

Often the planners and the practitioners in the government romanticise the maze of numbers and feel contented when the numbers are on an upward slope for the solutions and on a downward slope for problems. In the race to achieve numeric targets, some of the key qualitative processes get ignored often leading to misrepresentation of the actual picture against those numbers.

Processes like commitment from leadership, political non-interference, collective decision-making, lowered corruption, people's satisfaction levels are often ignored in everyday lives, which in the long run turn out to be irritants and also reason for people to make anti-incumbent choices.

Below are some of the mechanisms illustrated, which could be implemented to measure performance beyond numbers:

i. Based on similar lines as Transparency International, an index on unfair practices could be set up in Uttar Pradesh (division or district-wise) to capture and remedy corruption problems in the region.

ii. Develop a District Magistrate Feedback System on the functioning of the DM's office to assess levels of political interference or non-interference.

iii. Set up Public Forums in each district to provide feedback on the involvement (quantitative plus qualitative) in district-level policy and decision making processes.

iv. Monitor MLAs'/Ministers' field exposure, both through the number of visits as well as the quality of those visits.

v. Set up Legislature Capacity Building Centre at the state level to coach the elected members on people management, collective decision-making processes etc.

Empowering Government Officials

Basic human nature strives for empowerment and freedom in any institutional structure. Be it the government or private institutions, every employee gets motivated by systems and procedures which give them more autonomy, make them more accountable and gives them incentives for performance. In addition, skills and knowledge development is the core of building confidence and credibility.

Uttar Pradesh is no different than any other state or even national government in terms of low motivation level, poor accountability systems, with practically no system of incentivisation. With nearly 16 lakh employees at different grades, the state has very limited facilities and commitment towards setting up robust HR systems for its own employees.

Autonomy to work is one of the most important ingredients to deliver public service mandates and unfortunately this is the aspect that has been marred by day-to-day political interference, rigid scheme structures, and 'one size fits all' approach in planning. Even the most empowered IAS fraternity feels squeezed and helpless before the overpowering and invisible 'System'. Interestingly, there are examples where the officials themselves have beaten the system to show exemplary performance in governance and administration; however, these examples became islands of excellence and were never able to replicate themselves primarily because of the low autonomy in the system.

Accountability is the next important feature that often bottlenecks development programmes. Often accountability adorns a negative connotation and is confused with penalisation; however, accountability is a mechanism to track the final person or a team that is responsible for the outcome (whether good or bad). Incentivisation thus becomes an important tool to institutionalise accountability mechanisms and also a motivating force to perform beyond the 'call of duty'.

Task Force Model is a very successful model practiced across the world to deliver quick and high quality projects and programmes. Even in Uttar Pradesh, Task Force model had been tried out in the past for planning, budgeting and implementation of some special schemes. Unfortunately, such task forces converted into full-fledged departments and therefore killed the very spirit of the Task Force. The model is fairly simple and effective with some of the following features and benefits:

i. Officers of different levels from different departments are selected to join a Task Force. The selection is often unbiased and based on competence and experience of the officer in the particular field.

ii. The structure of the Task Force is relatively flat and people are assigned work streams in their areas of competence. There is a specific time-limit to complete the task with clear outcomes and deliverables.

iii. Generally, Task Forces function directly under the Chief Ministers leading to fast decision-making and execution. It also indicates government's priorities and preferences and therefore the subjects of Task Forces need to be carefully chosen.

iv. Members of the Task Forces often enjoy these tenures as it takes them out from their mundane departments, and make them enjoy a high learning curve by interacting with the best subject experts nationally and internationally. Also, the tenure and seniority in the parent department does not get affected.

v. The Task Forces generally enjoy a fairly high degree of autonomy as they are free from departmental pressures. Also, the accountability quotient is very high because of high visibility and high priority of the government.

Credibility and confidence in any human being can only come from well-updated skills and knowledge. Even some of the best of the government officials feel helpless when their own team members are poorly equipped in latest skills, understanding and knowledge of the subject. Learning and Development (L&D), more commonly known as in-service training, has always been a low-priority for state and national governments. A few institutions do exist to deliver L&D; however, the massive scale and periodicity at which it needs to be delivered, definitely needs a new thinking. Further, a new institution or a number of regional institutions is not the solution for an already burdened state exchequer.

A number of approaches are possible to expand L&D in the state for all levels of the administration. A few are mentioned below:

i. Linking L&D with the incentivisation methods for government officials. Special and prestigious training programmes, interaction with the leading personalities and global institutions, employee exchange programme with other states or countries could be designed for meritorious employees at all grades or levels.

ii. The new universities and institutions being set up in the state under Central or state laws should have mandatory provisions of training government staff. For example, private universities being set up under the State Private University Act, could be mandated and funded for continuously training government officials.

iii. The departments should be incentivised for creating training calendars for the employees and running relevant programmes for their staff. Autonomy to create special budgets should be given for the same.

iv. Allowing departments to access global accreditation like Global Development Learning Network, ISO standards etc.

Enhancing the E-governance Experience

E-governance is the savviest feature to enter government administration in India over the last decade. With a nearly Rs 50,000 crore ($10 billion) commitment from the Central and state governments towards e-governance, the subject is largely less understood.

Most of the states and their departments having huge budgets for e-governance are still far away from the concept and are merely digitising their paper information. Now, a 'note-sheet' is typed and printed through computer before it starts its journey through multiple desks, departments and hierarchy. Quantitative data is maintained in huge excel files and often the 'computer programmer' becomes the 'chief planner' of any department.

Figure 2.1

Two-Lens Approach to Select e-Gov Project

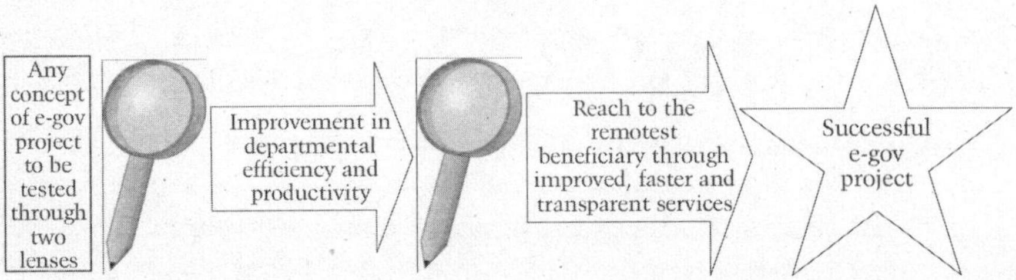

Without doubt there are some remarkable stories in e-governance, which have transformed some of the largest systems in the country like income tax, rail reservation, MCA-21 etc. However, there are important lessons to be learnt from each of the examples.

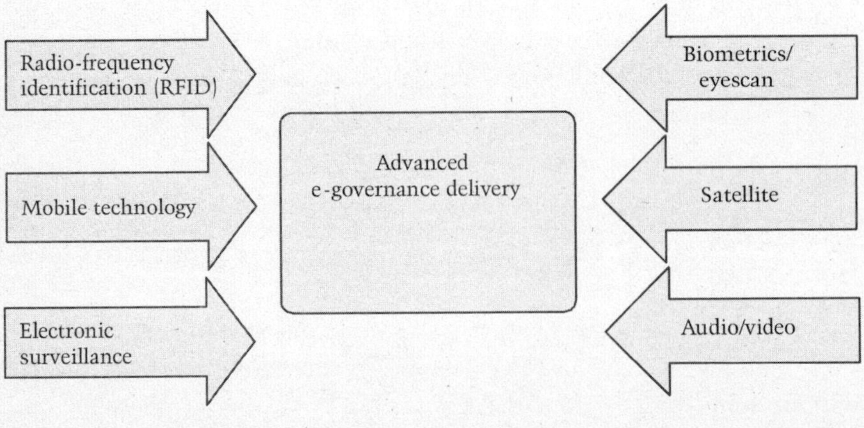

Uttar Pradesh also has a big mandate for e-governance and almost every department now has a website; however, a random check on most websites reveals outdated and unusable information, poor design and negligible interactivity.

The next level of e-governance is the use of multiple technologies like radio-frequency identification (RFID), mobile technology, biometrics, electronic surveillance and integration between them to deliver 360° services to the citizens, businesses and other government agencies.

Overhauling the Police System and Ensuring Speedy Justice

There is an overwhelming literature on reforms in police and the justice system in Uttar Pradesh. Some of the literature is written by serving senior officers and some by retired officers of the system and each one of them is 'spot-on' in diagnosing the ailments in the system. The important ones are:

- Slow pace of modernisation of the force.
- Archaic training and lag against the emergence of new forms of crimes. Inability to handle pressures and poor work-life balance.
- Poor career management.
- Political interference and alignments based on caste.
- False crime reporting and upward management.

The logical extension of the police system is the justice system, which also is plagued by delays, corruption and nepotism. The backlog in the judiciary is not of a few years but of a couple of decades. Further, the common person is fleeced by the monopoly of the lawyers' lobby who encash on the information asymmetry emerging through archaic laws, multiple interpretations and their own quest for survival. To sum up, the security and justice machinery for the common person is the scariest to access and many term it as a 'black hole'.

Table 2.1

The Seven Supreme Court Directives: Uttar Pradesh's Turnout

No.	*Summary of Directives*	*Status of Uttar Pradesh (2010)*
1	Constitute a State Security Commission • Ensure that state government does not exercise unwarranted influence or pressure on the police. • Lay down broad policy guideline and • Evaluate the performance of the state police	Partially achieved
2	Ensure that DGP is appointed through merit based transparent process and secure a minimum of two years	Partially achieved
3	Ensure that police officers on official duties are also provided a minimum of two years	Not achieved
4	Separate the investigation and law & order functions of the police	Partially achieved
5	Set up Police Establishment Board (PEB) to decide transfers, postings, promotions, and other service related matters of police officers below the rank of DSP and make recommendations on postings and transfers above the rank of DSP	Partially achieved
6	Set up Police Complaints Authority (PCA) at state level to inquire into public complaints against police officers of and above the rank of DSP in cases of serious misconduct, including custodial death, grievous hurt or rape in police custody and at district levels to inquire into public complaints against the police personnel below the rank of DSP in cases of serious misconducts	Not achieved
7	Set up National Security Commission at the Union level to prepare a panel for selection and placement of Chiefs of Central Police Organisations (CPO) with a minimum tenure of two years	Centre's responsibility

In 2006, the Supreme Court directed all states to comply with seven-binding directives that would kick-start reform; however, even after five years of the order, the compliance report (CHRI, 2010)[1] shows a dismal performance for most of the states in the country including Uttar Pradesh.

It is fairly evident that measures which affect the common person have been completely ignored and directives where institutions are required have been partially met.

1. *http://www.humanrightsinitiative.org/programs/aj/police/india/initiatives/seven_steps_to_police_reform.pdf*

It is interesting to note that even directives from the country's supreme judiciary are complied with in a lackadaisical manner and the agencies responsible remain indifferent to such orders. The reasons could be many and arguments could stretch to either side; however, it would be worthwhile to explore the implementation design of such orders, if any were there. Courts usually deliver some utopian judgements with the expectation that some-one in government would put together the implementation and that is where we falter!

Suppose all the directives of the Supreme Court are fully implemented in Uttar Pradesh—would that mean an improved police system and address some of the ailments diagnosed earlier in the section? Maybe partially. Some of the larger issues of police-political nexus, modernisation, training and development may need some different kind of directives. Directives and strategies like:

i. Creating a different cadre to provide security cover to politicians. Also stricter rules in allocation of security cover.

ii. Incentivisation for registering and solving cases. Also, providing alternatives to people in case a particular police station (PS) is non-cooperative, for example, launching complaint in a PS outside the jurisdiction, online/sms complaints etc.

iii. Latest training and cross-deputation for DSP and below through exchange programmes with national and international governments.

iv. Financing modernisation and ease/transparency in procurement. Revisiting the current procurement system. Seeking expert help from agencies like the World Bank, consultants etc.

Needless to say, there are a few in the system who have brought in innovation and set examples of change; however, the attempts have been either cosmetic or too niche, limited to academic discussions. The people of Uttar Pradesh are still awaiting a deep dive overhaul into the security systems in the state.

Judicial Reforms

The police system is often consumed in keeping pace with the justice system and compromising on the time and energy needed to maintain law and order and investigations. The current dispute resolution system is plagued by numerous inefficiencies both by design and by act.

Apart from Supreme Court, high courts and subordinate courts, there are other forms of settling disputes like conciliation, mediation, arbitration, Lok Adalats, *panchayats*, family courts and women's courts. Unfortunately, the backlog of cases, vacancies in the system, low productivity and poor use of the technology are reasons enough for the inefficiencies in dispute resolution thereby creating substantial pressure on the police system and widening of the 'black hole' described earlier.

Many of the supply-side constraints are by design. Lok Adalats can only get referral cases from other courts and cannot accept a fresh case. *Panchayats* do not have competent and rational decision-making process, making them less dependable on matters of issuing judgments. Similarly, arbitration under its Act is highly technical and complicated providing a legal trap for the unwary.

Further, the demand side also has a unique situation where estimates show that the number of government litigation crowds out private citizen from civil courts. This primarily arises out of appeals, which have 'automaticity'. The decision to appeal is generally taken at the bottom of government's decision-making authority while to nullify the same it has to go all the way to the top. Though the courts have started penalising for making frivolous appeals, it is for the respective government department to judge and filter out frivolous appeals at its own level. This would significantly reduce the burden of courts and devote more time to private citizens and cases.

In addition, the judicial reform process can be categorised into primarily three layers, with specific interventions needed at each level:

1. Statutory law reform: Estimates indicate that there might be about 2,500 Central laws and about 25,000 state laws existing in India.

However, whatever may be the number, there are three clear elements to statutory law reform (Judicial Reforms, Bibek Debroy[2]):

i. Weeding out old and dysfunctional elements in legislation (e.g. the earliest Central statute dates back to 1836—Bengal Indigo Contracts Act and Bengal Districts Act).

ii. Unification and harmonisation—simplify, merge different statutes, which overlap between ministries, departments both at the Central and state level. Also harmonisation is important from point of view of equity; for example, 92 per cent of population in the unorganised labour market does not have any significant labour legislations whereas the balance 8 per cent population in the organised market has overprotective and rigid laws. Setting up of state level law commissions could be a way in this direction.

iii. Reducing state intervention: integrate more than 25,000 state level statutes spread across the country.

2. Administrative law reform: There are no estimates of subordinate legislations of Central/state government ministries/departments like the number of rules, regulations, orders, and instructions that form the basis of innumerable appeals and litigations in courts. The government would have to take conscious steps to reduce the number of appeals, avoid taking cases to the judiciary, which are inter-departmental, and proactively simplify procedures using e-governance.

3. Judicial reforms: There is a backlog of about 2.3 crore cases in different courts of India (20,000 in SC, 30 lakh in HCs and 2 crore in LCs) and if the number of new cases exceeds the ones disposed, the situation gets further worsened. There is plenty of literature for improving productivity of courts and clearing the backlog, unfortunately 'implementation' is the missing link in the chain of recommendations.

---

2. Debroy, Bibek (n.d.). "Judicial Reforms: Law and Contract Enforcement", *http://www.mayin.org/ajayshah/A/Debroy2.pdf*

Though the greater push is needed at an overall judiciary level, the state can play a proactive role by taking some steps to help the judiciary function efficiently. This would in turn lessen the burden of the government itself. Some of the items to consider are:

i. Empower local level alternate dispute resolution systems e.g. capacity building drive for *panchayats* or set up competent Panchayat Judicial Cells.

ii. Establish 'appeal filter' system in government departments.

iii. Establish a state government arbitration system with magisterial powers.

iv. Set up a strong judiciary support system to help courts improve their efficiency and productivity. Systems of easy access for citizens to courts, lawyer assistance for the poor, technology based data and information.

3 Remodelling the Growth Pillars

Core Sectors and Services

The economy, infrastructure and social welfare and security net are the three core pillars in remodelling growth in any society. Further, each of these three is a necessary condition for development and a low priority on any of them can create a void in the society.

The primary purpose here is to relook at each of the sectors and identify the 'critical gaps' and a 'starting point' of the journey, which is closely aligned, to the new vision and create simple, doable models to unleash the potential in each sector. For example, each sector in each district could have different starting points and therefore start the journey differently towards better provisioning, better quality of provisioning and equity in provisioning.

Figure 3.1

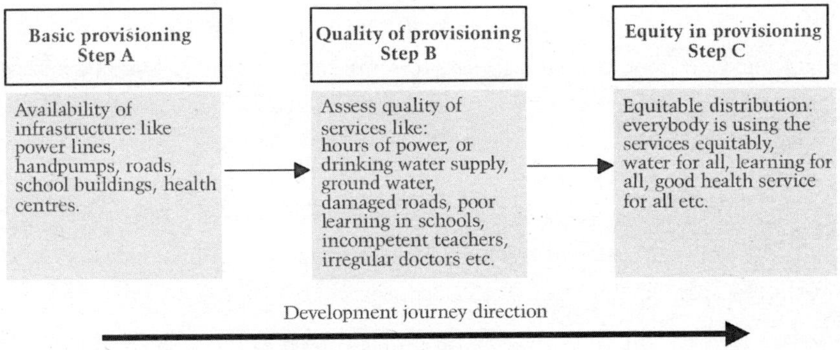

Enhancing the Economic Security

Economy in Uttar Pradesh has often borne the brunt of corruption, multiple regulations, political vendettas and non-transparent systems. The low growth rates, low per capita, poor FDI inflows have remained a feature for many years. Though at some points these indices might have shown a brighter side of the state, the day to day lives of farmers, traders, entrepreneurs and individuals have remained unaffected for decades, clearly evident through:

- poor agricultural yield,
- uncompetitive pricing,
- confusing land titles,
- complex trade policies and the *raj* of the middlemen,
- politically motivated investment policies and
- low and inequitable banking and FI penetration.

Having said that, it is heartening to see that the people have not lost hope and still believe in the system and its ability to deliver the best for them. The industry still is waiting for an opportunity to invest heavily in the state. It therefore becomes our duty to channelise the energies around three core areas and give people a platform to exploit their talent and potential.

Improving Agriculture Productivity

The comparative advantage of Uttar Pradesh in agriculture is unparalleled and could be compared to some of the most advanced nations in the world. The quality of soil, the weather conditions, the availability of human resources and the consumption within the state could beat many developed countries. However, even with such rich resources, agriculture in Uttar Pradesh has not been able to contribute much to the state economy—nearly 60 per cent of the workforce is in the agriculture sector, which contributes only 30 per cent to the economy.

The average yield of major crops has been considerably low. There have been declining growth rates of production and productivity for all crops, sharp year-to-year fluctuation in food grain output and total agriculture produce, indicating high dependence on monsoons even though the state has a high proportion of cultivated area irrigated.

Box 3.1

Major Constraints Inhibiting Agricultural Growth

- Small and fragmented size of holdings.
- Lack of proper management and maintenance of surface irrigation system for reaping the benefit of maximum potential.
- Decline in public investment in agriculture.
- Inadequate research and development.
- Underdeveloped credit flow and institutional finance.
- Inadequate participation of private sector in the commercialisation of agricultural sector.

Source: UP Human Development Report 2007.

As outlined in Box 3.1, the factors constraining the farmer in terms of land preparation, crop monitoring during growing period, help in harvesting, transportation, logistics and prompt payment on agreed terms are critical for higher productivity and yield, and thereby rise in income for farmers.

Like many other states, Uttar Pradesh also has taken strides in reforming land policies, titles, ceiling on landholdings, renting etc., with multiple legislations; however, the implementation has suffered in the hands of ineffective officials and powerful landowners. The focus should shift to cleaning up multiple policy constructs, overlaps and conflicts and implementing directed policies to help farmers and labourers.

In order to rejuvenate the agriculture market economy, the government would have to take some big but doable steps. Some of them could be:

i. Revisit land reforms by removing distortion. Give the liberty to SC landowners to make choices to sell or lease in case they want to shift from farming.

ii. Lower the entry barriers in the agriculture market. Modify restrictions on procurement, processing and marketing of agricultural produce.

iii. Create vertically coordinated supply chains to eliminate inefficiencies in agricultural marketing that arise due to multilayer intermediaries.

iv. Build tripartite models between farmer cooperatives, private sector and agricultural institutions to boost productivity, using private sector's technology and marketing, agriculture institution's research and insights and collective strength of cooperative farming.

v. Build a system for 'option contracts' for farmers so that when the open market prices are higher than contract prices, they get open market price and when it is lower then they get the contract price.

Prioritising and Organising Trade and Investment

Industrial investment, growth in trade are levers to generate more employment, increase earning levels of people and push tertiary sector along with the primary sector.

Uttar Pradesh is an agricultural economy. Two-thirds of the workforce is engaged in agriculture. The state has not seen much diversification into manufacturing and services sector, which in other parts of the country are the primary drivers of growth. Interestingly, Uttar Pradesh being a low-income state has also seen low unemployment rates; however, the quality of employment had been poor with low returns and poor wages. Also, Uttar Pradesh's employment is concentrated in low productivity sector, with nearly 96 per cent in the informal/unorganised sector. The entire 60 per cent agricultural workforce is in the unorganised sector.

The government has to be conscious of the fact that inherently people are agrarian in nature and investments in services like IT, ITES would not directly impact labour productivity. Growth in services sector, largely concentrated in NOIDA region should not be indicative of growth and policies of overall Uttar Pradesh, because NOIDA is a result of an organic growth of the NCR region and does not represent larger population of Uttar Pradesh.

Uttar Pradesh would have to adopt a new strategy of focussed investments in agricultural and informal sector and make it more organised and productive. Even investment in industrial sector has to be prioritised in sectors that have backward and forward linkages to the agriculture and informal sector. The natural growth of services sector would continue to happen from education, health, banking, roads and other business services.

Below are some illustrated models to prioritise trade and investment policies:

Figure 3.2

COC Model

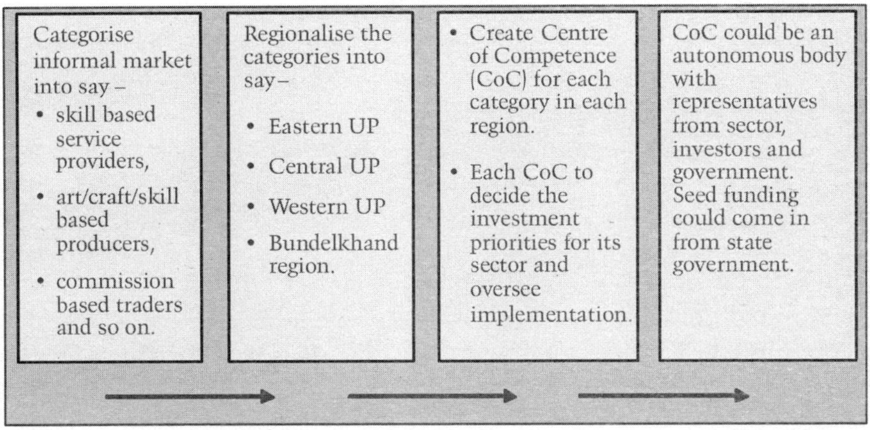

Figure 3.3

Value Chain Model

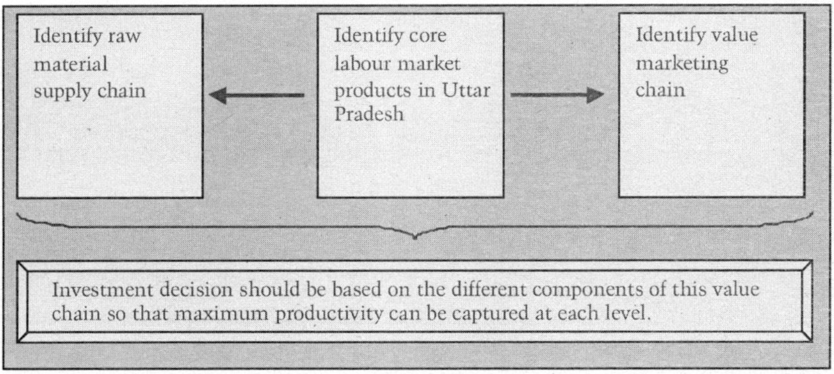

Industrialisation in Uttar Pradesh needs to be mandated by the choice of people's skills, services and trade and should be balanced and prioritised across regions.

Rejuvenating Financial Access and Services

Uttar Pradesh has a low penetration of banking and financial services with nearly one bank per 19,000 persons compared to one bank per 15,000 in India, which itself is also very low compared to say Brazil which has one bank per 8,000 persons or USA having one bank per 4,000 persons. There is still a large prevalence of informal loans, traditional moneylenders, poor record of repayments, poor saving and investment opportunities, and complex documentation/procedures to access banking. Leave aside small and marginal farmers and traders, industrial credit is also extremely low. Apart from NABARD, other financial institutions draw cold feet in Uttar Pradesh.

Without active financial markets, the state would continue to depend on external aid and Central funds. Also, an active financial market is needed to boost sub-sectoral growth, related to the financial sector like financial education, commodity exchanges, insurance markets, credit rating etc.

Financial markets is always a 'chicken and egg' situation and is largely dependent on willingness of people to move money and their risk appetite. The more people trade, use credit, repay, save/invest, more the market becomes active and attractive—something inherently active in Gujarat. Therefore, the government would have to force-simulate an environment by setting up accessible institutions and instruments in order to trigger excitement in the market. Some of the measures could be:

- Commodity exchanges: Set up regional commodity exchanges, which could be an extension of agriculture institutions with extensive education and training around the subject.
- Insurance kiosks: These kiosks could be set up at block level or near trading *mandis* with some mandatory insurance schemes, which could also be subsidised by the government. A couple of essential products like health insurance, disability insurance could be mandated.
- Micro-investments: Banks and MFIs should actively extend short-term investment opportunities and demonstrate real gains (gains adjusted to inflation) in short period to infuse confidence amongst users.

- Mobile banking: Not to be confused with 'cell-phone' banking. This is primarily to make banks reach the consumers rather than consumers searching for banks.

Enriching the Infrastructure Support

Infrastructure—be it power or utilities, roads or logistics—is one of the hottest topics in the country. A $500 billion investment is planned in the country under the Twelfth Plan. No matter what the share of Uttar Pradesh is, in the country strategy, Uttar Pradesh should systematically create a world class infrastructure around its people's priorities and align it with national development.

Uttar Pradesh urgently needs solutions around power, intensive and quality road and transport networks and quick answers around urbanisation. This prioritisation in no way undermines the importance of other infrastructure priorities like airports, special economic zones (SEZs), railways, airports, clean energy etc. However, as mentioned earlier, the choice of sectors is only around the need of the general public in order to make their lives simpler, happier and more productive.

Power: Improving Distribution and Tariff Collection

Uttar Pradesh urgently needs stable power generation capacities, a robust distribution system and efficient tariff collection mechanism. In addition, alternate energy resources like wind and solar are to be exploited in the state.

Since the mid-1990s, multiple power sector reforms have been initiated both Centrally as well as state-wise. However, the experience across states has not been encouraging with no superlative model emerging either in reorganisation of state electricity boards or improving efficiency of the distribution system. Unfortunately, the power sector has progressed through decade of trial and plenty of error, e.g. private investments in generation have not materialised primarily because of the poor financial health of the distribution system. Further, though the Electricity Act, 2003 delicensed generation, issues related to land acquisition, fuel linkages continued to be major bottlenecks for the private sector.

Interestingly, Uttar Pradesh has made some strides in power generation with an investment of nearly Rs 64,000 crore during the Eleventh Plan and is attempting to add nearly 10,500 MW additional power capacity by 2012 through its network of Uttar Pradesh Rajya Vidyut Utpadan Nigam Ltd. (UPRVUNL), Uttar Pradesh Jal Vidyut Nigam Ltd. (UPJVNL) and some private sectors which together are currently generating around 10,000 MW. It is estimated that this production would nearly meet the generation gap in the state.

The latest thinking in the reform agenda, Restructured Accelerated Power Development and Reform Programme (R-APDRP), is laying stress on the parameter of improving collection efficiency and controlling distribution losses. For example, if the state exceeds a percentage of collection efficiency, the entire loan amount from Central government would convert into a grant—a major policy change!

It is high time for Uttar Pradesh to leverage upon this opportunity and make some real strides in overhauling the infrastructure to control distribution losses and improve tariff collections.

The recent Distribution Reform Upgrade and Management project between GoI and USAID has demonstrated several key initiatives, which could be replicated across DISCOMs in Uttar Pradesh. A few initiatives to overhaul power distribution and tariff collection are:

- Conduct a comprehensive energy audit for the state to segregate and pinpoint the commercial and technical losses and prioritise projects and plan the network for future growth in population as well as by envisioning their different needs of electricity.
- Install Distribution Automation systems such as outage management system, trouble-call management system, metering, billing, collection and financial system.
- Update the infrastructure knowledge of distribution system and redesign the network for efficiency through technical assistance and training at different levels like SEB, DISCOMS, distribution circles and feeders, rural electricity cooperatives etc.
- Remove the policy glitches in engaging private contractors to take on phase-wise distribution management at the distribution circle or feeder level.

Roads: Ensuring Last Mile Connections

Roads are the backbone of any economy, more so in an agriculture economy. Over the last few years, the aggregate indices on road and transport in Uttar Pradesh might have been encouraging; however, the last mile connectivity remains a widespread bottleneck. In order to resolve the problem of connecting the final habitations, a widespread problem across the country, GoI launched the Pradhan Mantri Gram Sadak Yojana (PMGSY) in 2000, which now has completed a decade. The upside of this scheme was that it was neutral to any political colours and has been supported over the years by different governments in the Centre as well as the states.

Uttar Pradesh was the only state in the country with one of the highest number of small habitations categorised in 1,000+, 500+, 250+ populations. Nearly 23 per cent of the state was spread out in such habitations and this was almost three times to its closest Andhra Pradesh. Therefore the starting point for Uttar Pradesh was itself daunting with nearly 37 per cent habitations uncovered by 'all-weather roads' (Table 3.1).

Over the last 10 years, the state has been able to reduce the gap by a mere 4 per cent and the current gap stands at nearly 33 per cent. Even if we add the habitations where roads have been upgraded, nearly 26 per cent or 55,000 habitations still remain uncovered. This effectively means that even in 2011, nearly 4-5 crore people out of 18-20 crore population do not have road connectivity.

The government at the state level would have to take some radical steps to improve its implementation speed, especially in the road sector. Some of them could be:

- Set up 18 Divisional Level Road Implementation Councils to plan, procure and monitor road implementation work.
- Align the Road Development mandate with NREGA and other schemes to augment and channelise funds at the district level.
- Create an Operations and Maintenance Fund for sustaining the habitation roads after the five-year mandatory contractor's responsibility of maintaining the road. Use the fund and set up a mechanism to ensure that there is continuity and incentive for the contractor to maintain those roads for 25 to 30-year periods.

Table 3.1

No.	*State*	*Total Habitations in the 1000+, 500+, 250+ and 0-249 Category as of 1-4-2000*	*Uncovered Habitations as on 1-4-2000*	*% Uncovered*	*Covered so far by New Construction*	*Balance Remaining*	*% Balance*	*Progress Rate Over 10 Years (%)*	*Habitations with Upgraded Roads*
1	Uttar Pradesh	216562	79976	36.93	8914	71062	32.81	11	15399
2	Andhra Pradesh	70894	4716	6.65	1547	3169	4.47	33	10287
3	Tamil Nadu	65831	2421	3.68	1523	898	1.36	63	7462
4	Maharashtra	61266	7392	12.07	1225	6167	10.07	17	8258
5	Karnataka	60108	484	0.81	389	95	0.16	80	9924

Source: *www.omms.nic.in* on PMGSY.

Urban Development and Affordable Housing

Uttar Pradesh remains primarily a rural state with an urban share of population of nearly 22 per cent, as opposed to national average of more than 31 per cent. Going by this trend, even by 2030, less than 30 per cent of its population would live in urban settings.

It is widely known that economic development/growth go hand in hand with increased urbanisation. The key reason for this relationship between GDP growth and urbanisation is that the increased density of urban population produces scale benefits that boost productivity, which in turn enhances productivity, a virtuous cycle. Uttar Pradesh has not been able to draw on this growth dynamic to the maximum given most of its populace currently resides in the countryside.

Uttar Pradesh does have few major cities like Lucknow, Kanpur, Agra, etc., which can play a leading role in the state's growth renewal. A quick look at their recent growth rate reveals encouraging signs e.g., Kanpur and Lucknow both grew in excess of 8 per cent between 1999-2005. However, a closer look indicates that state activity (public spending) was the prime driver of growth as opposed to pure business dynamism.

This is because urban centres do not necessarily lead to faster growth; they merely represent necessary preconditions that by no means are sufficient. Cities lead growth process by providing access to key services like housing, transport, water, sewage, etc. Thus, helping their residents to contribute their maximum energy towards growth.

Uttar Pradesh should take a multi-pronged approach to utilise potentially beneficent impact of urban centres in propelling the state's economic growth. While on the one hand it should improve the service delivery levels on core services, on the other hand it should invest in key regions to stimulate growth and reap rich benefits.

Bringing up urban infrastructure to meet basic hygiene level necessitates significant investment expenditure. Estimates indicate that Lucknow would need to spend Rs 76,000 crore and Kanpur Rs 63,000 crore between 2010 and 2030 on core urban infrastructure services like roads, sewage, water, etc.

Clustering strong economic linkages across co-located cities, could play a powerful role in giving boost to the economy by enlarging the size of the market, provide access to key infrastructural facilities like airports, ports, etc., and ability to tap into core production factors like skilled workforce. It is important to realise that clusters work on the central premise of enhancing and realising inherent growth potential of cities, which exist because of natural/legacy reasons. The fact that clusters work as catalyst to bring hidden potential into actual reality, they have a very good chance in succeeding as opposed to some of the other cited wayouts like creating new cities, which first have to establish their economic rationale.

A well developed mode of transport (road, rail) is generally found to have maximum 'bang for the buck' in terms of increased economic activity and growth. The Uttar Pradesh government should look at forming economic clusters atleast among the following cities, Ghaziabad-Meerut-Agra and Lucknow-Kanpur-Allahabad-Varanasi, by constructing 8-10 lane expressways between them. This would generate immense economic activity and employment opportunities.

A case in point is the about to be completed KMP expressway (Kundli-Manesar-Palwal) in Haryana. This 135 km expressway connects all the satellite towns of Delhi, running all the way from North to South of Haryana. The state government plans to build 7-8 theme cities, on themes like education city, biotech city, IT city, etc., along the expressway to catalyse economic development. If initial impact is to be gauged in terms of realty prices, the project has already become a big hit, with real estate prices rising between 100-200 per cent since 2007. It is important to appreciate that being in one state such developments also do not require coordination amongst multiple states' agencies.

Though clustering of existing cities through faster/reliable mode of transport can play a key role in kick-starting and accelerating economic development, the contentious issue of land acquisition needs to be tackled urgently and equitably to minimise the risk of project over-runs and delays.

Affordable Housing

Providing affordable housing to the lower strata of population is a burning issue for the country in general and Uttar Pradesh in particular.

Roughly 30 per cent of Uttar Pradesh's urban population lives in slums. This is way higher than the 22 per cent for India as a whole. The contrast becomes all the more stark when we observe that Uttar Pradesh was just 21 per cent urbanised in 2001 as opposed to 28 per cent for all-India. Thus, although Uttar Pradesh has much smaller urban population, a significant percentage live in slums.

There is a massive gap in the affordability of housing by lowest earning deprived segment and the market price of houses for them. The price to affordability ratio is roughly between 4-5 times i.e., the actual price is about 4-5 times to what people can afford. Given the magnitude of the problem and the fact that common people, if left to themselves, would not be able to afford housing makes it imperative for state intervention.

Since the key issue is lack of affordability, the state can follow a combination of two main policies—increase affordability and/or decrease housing prices. In what follows, we shall deliberate on the pros and cons of each with a view to bring out an optimal and feasible approach. Two ways to increase affordability are:

1. Loan/interest subsidy, capital grants to the desired beneficiary.
2. Cross-subsidisation: One interesting model of cross-subsidisation being implemented is the Sukhobrishti project in Kolkata by West Bengal Housing Infrastructure Development Corporation Ltd. wherein a private developer is constructing 20,000 affordable housing units for low income/middle income groups in lieu of 50 acre commercial land at subsidised rates. This has twin benefits: on the one hand the state is able to develop affordable housing, on the other, it has resulted in expansion of quality office space, which would result in economic activity.

Though a lot of attention has been given to fine-tuning such cross-subsidisation mechanisms, it has shown limited success. One key problem is that it results in self-reinforcing problems. That is, if you create more affordable houses for today's poor population, it will result in more migration and thus further the need for more houses and so on. Therefore, a direct loan subsidy through tie-ups with a financial institution is a better approach.

Another option to resolve for high migration and therefore higher demand for affordable housing is to develop new cities based on themes like education, health care, IT etc. These cities should have access to all basic facilities like affordable housing where people can move in from other cities and rural areas. This can not only alleviate the housing shortage but also help in easing infrastructural/environmental and societal pressure on existing urban centres. The construction of four new economic cities in Saudi Arabia is a testimony to this idea. Envisioned at a cost of USD 60 billion, once complete, the cities will house 4-5 million people and contribute USD 150 billion to the Saudi economy. The four Arabian cities, though integrated and self-sufficient, have their respective axes, which will provide the necessary minimum thrust. Thus, while King Abdullah Economic City (KAEC) will focus on industrial and light manufacturing, Jazan Economic City (JEC) will focus on energy intensive industries. It is important that while these cities have a primary focus, there would be other activities as well. Thus, for e.g. KAEC will also offer prime office and mixed-use commercial space including a 14-hectare financial district, which will be region's biggest.

The idea is to establish a new city by carving out a niche value proposition, which takes it onto a self-reinforcing growth process. However, once that process is well entrenched, economic agents may sense opportunities in new activities, which were not 'planned' for. Unless it contradicts with the USP of the primary axes (say, manufacturing in a tourist city), the city should encourage and nurture these organic growth impulses.

Strengthening the Social Welfare and Security Net

Education, health and social security are the prime drivers towards ensuring productivity, stability and happiness in human beings. These are the sectors which cut across religion, caste and gender, and have a direct impact to bring about a striking change in the personality of every individual.

Education: Overhauling the System

Education in Uttar Pradesh has seen a downfall over the decades. Government schools have been reduced to instruments to execute constitutional mandate of education and only report quantitative numbers to justify their sustenance. Higher education institutions have just become training grounds to practise and enter politics, where academics is only limited to granting degrees. Just to remind that higher education is limited to only those who complete school education i.e., a large part of the students drop out of the school system (nearly 80%) and enter the labour market directly.

Leaving aside a few institutions like private schools, IITs, IIMs, the state is reeling under great pressure to create quality education provisioning for the masses. A radical approach is required to overhaul the system in the state.

School Education

Uttar Pradesh has one of the highest education budgets in the country. Even with such large investments, the poor outcome of the school system has been a cause of concern not only for policymakers but also for the public at large. These outcomes contribute to low economic growth, high failure rates, high out-of-age enrollment and a low skill base in the state.

Considerable research has been done to identify issues and different schemes and experiments have also been undertaken to address issues of enhancing learning levels, bridging gender and social gaps, teacher development and classroom processes. Even with large seale programmes and commitment through policies, little dent has been made to improve the overall quality of education in the state, quite evident through low education development index and human development index.

In recent years, the focus of policies and programmes has further shifted from inputs to outcomes for both children as well as teachers. Children and teachers are being considered as a unit for all the interventions as the issues of both are equally important and need remediation for them to perform as a well-oiled unit. It is important to look at a few children and teachers related issues before we discuss about solutions.

Child related Issues

Access to schools just does not mean physical access, but has a wider scope. It entails larger issues of safety, convenience, classrooms, seating, equity and private & public transport. Many of the issues of retaining children in schools have roots in the issues of access. Retention, linked to the achievement of children in schools, banks heavily on issues of availability of TLMs, books, libraries, availability of in-school remedial support, attractiveness of classrooms and teacher's behaviour. Similarly, achievement of children does not merely mean passing percentage but also means how well children are coping with minimum levels of learning in each grade, how processes of assessment and evaluation are getting administered, use of technology, linkages of curriculum with market or employment, awards, scholarships and recognition.

Teacher related Issues

The other integral component of the school is the teacher and it is imperative to also look at issues related to teachers with the same intensity as that of the children. Three broad issues with respect to teachers are identified as:

- professional development,
- incentive system and
- administrative support and convenience.

Professional development in the form of pre-service training, linked to present day curriculum; in-service training linked to operational difficulties; armament with the latest technology in child education and enhancement of academic qualifications are key issues related to capacity development of teachers. The key issues related to incentive system of teachers involve parity, realistic allowances, awards and recognitions. And finally, the administrative support system and convenience provided to the teachers is important to maintain their motivation and focus on academic matters rather than administrative matters. A healthy system of monitoring, evaluation, appraisal and feedback are important to sustain the core competency of teaching amongst teachers. Similarly, a well-trained cadre of education administrators is important to extend all possible convenience to the performance of teachers. Modern infrastructure and use of technology are critical in enhancing efficiency in the system.

Strategy for School Education Department

To deliver high quality services not only to children but also to teachers, the back-end system of education department and bureaucracy has to ensure a steady financing, quality recruitment, innovation, global networks and high quality research in education management. A three-pronged approach is necessary for the department:

1. Demand-side Assessment for Resolving Advanced Education Management Issues

To address advanced issues in terms of access, equity and quality, the department should focus on:

- Establishing linkages of transition between primary-middle-secondary school systems. Try and identify gaps, which have occurred by design, e.g. not enough seats available in the higher grade for the graduates of the lower grade.
- Conducting a systematic infrastructure diagnostic, like plotting the geographical location of schools, connectivity through road and transport, population base of the command area, safety, facilities at school, capacity to expand etc.
- Identifying education service points to different classes of population like below poverty line, SC, ST, OBC and above poverty line. Availability of private schools, tuition centres etc.
- Estimating realistic rather than norm based cost per child to extend good quality services to the underprivileged.
- Assessing the need of rationalisation of teachers and support services.
- Ensuring the right timing of distribution of books and TLM to the beneficiaries.
- Analysing the curriculum and content and linking it to the issue of its relevance. Identifying hard spots in the curriculum and linking them to a remedial system as a part of curriculum and pedagogy.
- Studying the pattern of teaching–learning in schools, to be directed to personal and professional development of the children rather than through test or examination.

- Appraising the teachers, based on competency and performance rather than qualifications and years of service. Also identify the scope for capacity/professional development within the system.

2. Public-Private Partnerships

The society and economy is rapidly shifting towards the regime where the government and private systems are leveraging each other's strengths to deliver a productive service to the society. The private systems are acknowledging the close linkage they need with the society and the public systems are acknowledging the need for specialists and professional systems to contribute to the large public service delivery system. With the success of PPP in public utility systems like energy, transport and infrastructure, it is time to establish similar organised systems in the education sector. PPPs in the education sector can happen in the following areas:

- Contracting for the delivery of education services.
- Private management of public schools.
- School infrastructure PPPs.
- Vouchers/subsidies.
- Private sector quality assurance.
- Public-private sector affiliation arrangements.
- Innovation and research PPPs.

3. Integration and Convergence of Different Schemes

Integration and convergence of different schemes and programmes directed towards the welfare of children and education can be done through:

- Scheme customisation for a specific target group under the overall policy framework in order to make a substantial impact in delivery. Time-bound and outcome orientation in the schemes would also lead to greater accountability in the system.

- Rationalisation of departments, sub-departments and people for efficient resource management and alignment of different schemes under each department to avoid scheme-conflict at the field level.
- Flexibility to be built-in to address regional needs and customisation. Schemes should have administrative decentralisation and autonomy to execute.

Higher Education

While school education establishes the basic credentials in children, the next level of education is about how useful it is in employment generation, informed decision-making and overall personality development useful for employment as well as entrepreneurship.

The Yashpal Committee Report (2009)[1] has done a complete diagnostic and prescription for higher education in India, also relevant to Uttar Pradesh in many respects and reforms would continue to happen in the University education at their own pace. However, there are steps which the state may initiate to catalyse the overall reforms; Uttar Pradesh should have some concrete aspirations over five years:

1. Develop outstanding universities/world class institutes, making Uttar Pradesh revive its old glory of a preferred destination for higher education. Also develop it as a centre for high quality research.
2. Create an easy framework for private sector participation with quality international and industry partnerships and strong faculty development systems.

A few clear action points in this direction could be:

i. Create a special Task Force to augment university reforms as being prescribed by Yashpal Committee Report.

ii. Launch big breakthrough initiatives like 'an education city', 'faculty exchange and deputation programmes', 'incentivisation of high quality research', 'global research conclaves' etc.

---

1. *http://www.academics-india.com/Yashpal-committee-report.pdf*

Unfortunately, the issues are fairly common across all these institutions—primarily poor quality of training and course curriculum, negligible linkages with rural population and private incentives to fleece patients.

3. Transparent financing mechanisms to remove the funding bottleneck both from the demand and supply side: During a health emergency, funding the critical care becomes a severe bottleneck both from the hospital side as well as the patient side. The unwanted nexus between government hospitals, local drug dealers and private nursing homes, the lack of funds to maintain equipments thereby their non-usability and inherent corruption to fleece the patient using the pretext of non-transparent rules and policies further aggravate the problems. The patients also face severe information asymmetry as well lack of financial cover for life-saving treatments.

A three-pronged approach is needed to address the burning issues in health care.

I. Expanding and modernising health care infrastructure

- Pilot a state-wide referral transport system including mobile and emergency health care.
- Unveil a modernisation plan for the existing PHCs, secondary and tertiary health centres.
- Expand technology health care through mobile and internet.

II. Raising the bar for high quality medical education and paramedic training

- Create SEZs for health care and medical education with private participation.
- Set up block and district level modern paramedic/nursing/lab assistant training centres.
- Incentivise meritorious staff and doctors by exposing them to international exchange programmes and training programmes.

III. Fair and transparent financing

- Create a health care liquid fund for free or low interest rate micro-loans to reduce the out-of-pocket expenditure by households.
- Establish advanced fiscal management system for effective distribution and fund utilisation.
- Launch a low-premium health care insurance scheme in partnership with private/public insurance companies using mobile and other technology platforms for maximum reach.

Social Security Net

Availability and confidence towards a robust safety net in any eventuality is one of the most prime concerns of any human being. Though the rich create their own net by proper investments, insurances, the poor are neither aware nor economically sensitive to plan for a security net. And rightly so, the dependence is largely upon government to take care of them in any eventuality.

The government on the other hand might have lofty ideas on creating such nets; however, the insensitivity during implementation and corruption create unmanageable holes in the net. Leave aside planned safety system like medicare, unemployment, disability cover, pension etc., even ad hoc compensations in the event of floods, earthquake, accidents are marred by rent-seeking and indifference of the officials.

Though there may be good systems to look at in advanced nations in Europe or America, we would have to create simple doable models in our conditions. The efficiencies of the private sector could be greatly leveraged to provide such safety covers. Insurance companies, banks, telecom companies can come together and develop simple instruments for the poor that could be subsidised by the government and NGOs plus civic bodies could play an evaluative role in the process.

A rich embodiment of knowledge exists in models around the world for social protection and nothing stops us from accessing that knowledge to implement in the state. Based on a safety net programme outlined by The World Bank (Box 3.2), Uttar Pradesh could also have a state level safety net programme which can be an answer to the current fragmented approach. The programme could have proprietary products and knowledge, toolkits for

Box 3.2

What is the Role of Safety Nets?

Safety nets are part of a broader poverty reduction strategy interacting with and working alongside of social insurance; health, education and financial services; the provision of utilities and roads and other policies aimed at reducing poverty and managing risk.

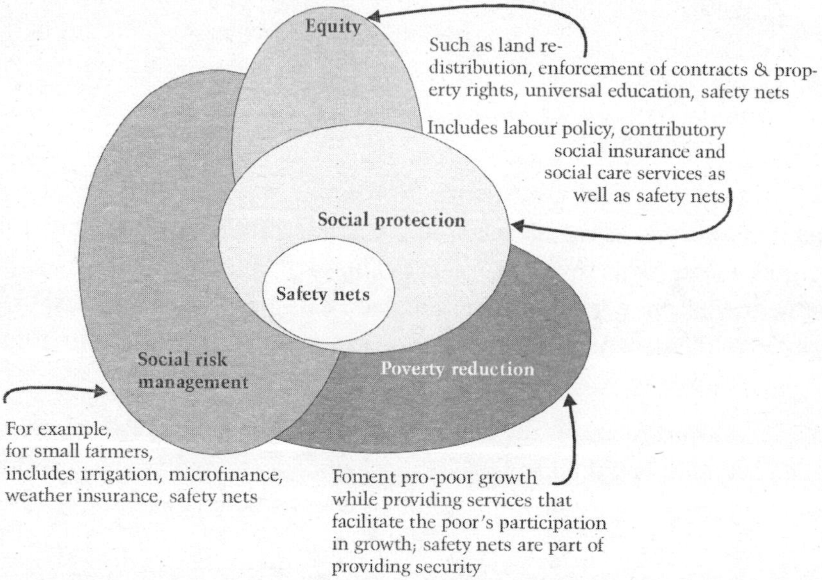

Safety net programmes can play four roles in development policy:

1. Safety nets redistribute income to the poorest and most vulnerable, with an immediate impact on poverty and inequality.
2. Safety nets enable households to make productive investments in their future that they may otherwise miss e.g., education, health, income generating opportunities.
3. Safety nets help households manage risk. At minimum, offsetting harmful coping strategies. At best, providing an insurance function which improves livelihood options.
4. Safety nets allow governments to make choices that support efficiency and growth.

Source: www.worldbank.org

diagnostics, impact evaluation, implementation primers, advanced training nuggets etc.

The programme can also integrate:

- Cash transfers and conditional cash transfer in the event of crisis like drought, floods, accidents etc.
- Food related programmes like mid-day meal, food ration cards, food aid in emergencies.
- Price and other subsidies like VAT exemptions, transport & storage subsidies etc.
- Public works schemes like MNERGA.
- Health care services like compensating providers for the revenue forgone.
- Education, electricity and housing like fee waivers, utility subsidy to farmers and free housing to poor.

Some of the action points on widening and deepening the social security net in Uttar Pradesh, could be:

- Set up a state level social security programme and set out a clear agenda for social security in the state. Important areas could be health care, old-age pensions, emergency relief, price subsidies, food security and housing.
- Align with Unique Identification Authority to integrate health, pension, conditional cash transfer to the people in the state.
- Also, set up an Aid-Coordination Cell to integrate and channelise all aid flowing into the state like Central government aid, multilateral aid, international NGO aid etc.

4 Summary and Key Recommendations

Undoubtedly, there are multiple sectors, multiple themes and multiple measures that need urgent attention and can vary in perspective; however, there are some core themes and sectors, which are undisputedly on everyone's agenda, and this study has discussed those themes. Below is a summary of the key focus areas discussed in the study and also ways to implement them. The reason and rationale for the recommenda-tions are already discussed in greater detail in the main body of the study.

The overall charter for the next government should be to:

- Create an environment of trust amongst people, and create simple, scalable, sustainable models of development.
- Create a sense of safety, security and justice in the common person by honestly reforming archaic institutions.

Governance Reforms

Governance reforms are not only about easing the services for the public, they are also about bringing in transparency and accountability in public services, empowerment of departments to take independent decisions and appropriately incentivising and rewarding those who trigger changes.

To achieve the above, the leadership has to initiate the following to rejuvenate government departments. The administration has to:

- Move away from mere numeric targets and achievements, and measure parameters like commitment from leadership, political non-interference, collective decision-making, lowered corruption, people satisfaction levels etc.

- Assess where the administration stands in terms of competency, convenience and accountability and make it more accessible to the common person.
- Empower government departments to enhance autonomy, accountability, confidence and credibility amongst government officials.
- Strengthen the existing models of bringing the government and people closer through simpler processes not only through the use of e-governance but integrating different technologies like mobile, RFID, biometrics, satellite, electronic surveillance and latest audio-visual systems.
- Bring path-breaking changes in police and security by prioritising functions like, investigations, law & order, VIP security cover, traffic; through incentivisation schemes, modernisation in training, international deputation and exchange programmes.
- Proactively help judiciary to improve its productivity by creating systems like Appeal Filter System, Panchayat Judicial Cells, Alternate Arbitration System.
- Redefine politics to become sensitive to people's choices and more collaborative policymaking.

In order to achieve the above objectives, simple doable steps can be initiated at the state level across departments:

- Set up three Task Forces under the Chief Minister with the multi-department officials to focus on selected governance reforms, economic development and social welfare.
- Implement a performance management matrix to incentivise officials in the non-IAS cadre.
- Make arrangements with private management colleges for training and development of officials in the non-IAS cadre. Meritorious ones to be trained outside country.
- Significantly cut down bureaucratic processes on basic citizen services like birth & death certificates, copies of land records etc.

- Implement an integrated technology solution using computers, mobiles, biometrics etc., for easy access to key government services.

Special initiatives have to be taken to improve the functioning of the police forces and ensure speedy judicial redressal for common public. Intiatives like:

- Dividing the police into three cadres of Investigations, Law & order and VIP security.
- Incentivising police stations for registering and solving cases. Establishing a system of launching complaint in a police station outside the jurisdiction, online/SMS complaints etc.
- Revisiting the current procurement system with help from agencies like the World Bank, consultants etc.
- Cross-deputation of officers (DSP and below) through exchange programmes with national and international governments.
- Empower local level alternate dispute resolution systems e.g. capacity building drive for *panchayats* or set up competent Panchayat Judicial Cells.
- Establish 'appeal filter' system in government departments.
- Establish a state government arbitration system with magisterial powers.
- Set up a strong judiciary support system to help courts improve their efficiency and productivity. Systems of easy access for citizens to courts, lawyer assistance for the poor, technology based data and information.

Moving beyond administrative and judicial reforms, it is also important to put together a system where politics also becomes fact based and constructive. Some of the measures in this direction could be:

- Setting up a District Magistrate Feedback System at the DM office level to monitor level of political interference.
- Launching a division/district-wise corruption index system on similar lines as Transparency International.

- Setting up a Public Forum in each district to provide feedback on the involvement of public (quantitative plus qualitative) in district level policy and decision-making processes.
- Launching a Field Visit Monitoring system for politicians and senior officials to review the field visits both quantitatively and qualitatively.
- Setting up Legislature Capacity Building Centre at the state level to coach the elected members on people management, collective decision-making processes etc.

Economic and Infrastructure Reforms

Economic reforms in Uttar Pradesh cannot be alienated from agriculture reforms in the state. Trade and investment policies in the state should be prioritised to augment agriculture productivity. Even infrastructure expansion and management should be focussed to enable last mile connectivity, continuous supply of power, water and other services to farmers and other allied industries. Some of the measures in this direction could be:

- Rejuvenating agriculture market economy by launching and implementing special policies towards land management, cooperatives, and marketing of produce e.g., creating vertically coordinated supply chains for better markteting, options contracts for securing prices and tripartite models between farmer co-ops, private sector and agriculture institutes for capacity enhancement and productivity.
- Evolving a new strategy to align trade and investment with agriculture and labour market to make it more organised and productive. Even investment in industries could have forward and backward linkages with the unorganised labour market.
- Force-stimulating the financial markets to trigger excitement among people towards wealth creation by the infusion of financial education, commodity exchanges, insurance markets, credit rating systems, micro-investments.

- Creating new models like Distribution Automation Systems and redesigning the network for efficiency in the power sector; establish Divisional Road Implementation Councils to speed up the last habitation connectivity backlog and set up Road O&M Fund.
- Develop two modern economic urban clusters like Ghaziabad-Meerut-Agra and Allahabad-Lucknow-Kanpur, and initiate a few theme based cities like education city, health city, IT city etc.

Some of the key action points in this direction could be:

Agriculture and Trade

- Setting up five regional Centres of Competence (CoC) to prioritise trade and investment. CoCs to manage vertically aligned agriculture supply chain to remove inefficiencies in marketing due to intermediaries. CoCs to categorise and organise informal market through prioritisation and targetted investment.
- Introducing a Farmer Cooperative Law to provide greater autonomy, decentralisation and flexibility to partner with private sector and knowledge development with agriculture institutions.
- Setting up regional commodity exchanges, as extension of agriculture institutions with extensive education and training around the subject.
- Each block to have insurance kiosks near trading *mandis* with adequate subsidy by government.

Infrastructure Development and Management

- Launching a state-wide Energy Audit to plug the gaps and plan the power network.
- Installing Distribution Automation Systems for outage management, automatic metering, billing and collection.
- Organising special technical trainings at different levels like SEB, Discoms, distribution circles and feeders, rural electricity cooperatives etc.

- Setting up 18 Divisional Level Road Implementation Councils to plan, procure and monitor road implementation work.
- Creating an Operations and Maintenance Fund for sustaining the habitation roads after the five-year mandatory contractor's responsibility of maintaining the road. Using the fund, set up a mechanism to ensure that there is continuity and incentive for the contractor to maintain those roads for 25 to 30-year periods.
- Clustering cities in east and west Uttar Pradesh like Lucknow, Kanpur, Allahabad and Varanasi as one cluster and Ghaziabad, Meerut and Agra as another to augment economic growth.
- Create a system of direct subsidy through tie-ups with financial institutions for housing loans and capital grants.
- Launching theme based cities like on education and health care and developing infrastructure for mainstream as well as allied industry growth. Also creating special provisions for housing, water, sanitation, waste management and transport.

Social Sector Reforms

Uttar Pradesh cannot afford to continue with a Human Development Index (HDI) which continues to be in the bottom quartile of the country. Education, health care, social security net are the key drivers for an improved HDI. In addition to the existing problems, new challenges are being witnessed in the form of demographic changes, equitable distribution and quality of services. Some major and urgent reforms are needed in the sector and these are:

- Redefining school education by moving to the new level of identifying needs related to children and teachers and solving advanced issues in equity, parity in learning with private schools, well updated cadre of teachers and education administrators. Actively pursuing the true spirit in private partnerships in the light of RTE Act rather than mere contractual arrangements.
- Making the state a preferred destination in higher education and health care by setting up 4-5 outstanding universities and world

class institutions and actively build human capacities in the state to deliver high quality health and education services.

- Revamping the current public health care system by launching a modernisation plan for primary health centres (PHCs), secondary and tertiary centres. Also ensuring availability of manpower at block and district level by recruiting and training the cadre of paramedics, nursing and lab assistants.
- Creating an integrated system of health care financing, subsidy and insurance both for practitioners and users.
- Ensuring a state level social security system to service pension, price subsidies, food security for poor & marginalised and for coordinating aid during emergencies.

Some of the urgent steps which need to be taken in education, health care and social security are:

Education

- Launching the country's first PPP policy in education to implement the Right to Education to ensure equitable and quality education for all.
- Setting up a state-wide education geographic information system (GIS) to monitor and plan education at all levels.
- Launching three big breakthrough initiatives in higher education:
  - Education city.
  - Faculty exchange programme.
  - Fund for high quality education research.
- Setting up an International Standard Accreditation Board to not only monitor the performance of higher education institutions but also help the students choose the most relevant courses for themselves.
- Allowing state universities to set up 'link programmes', 'twinning arrangements', 'distance learning arrangements' and 'study centres' with foreign universities.

Health Care

- A new state-wide referral health transport system including mobile and emergency health care.
- All primary, secondary and tertiary health centres to be covered under a State Modernisation Plan.
- Private sector to be invited to set up Technology Health Care through mobiles and internet.
- Special economic zoning for health care and medical education with private participation.
- Creating a Health Care Liquid Fund for free or low interest rate micro-loans to reduce the out-of-pocket expenditure by households.
- Launching Advanced Fiscal Management System for effective distribution and fund utilisation.
- Launching a low-premium Health Care Insurance Scheme.

Social Security

- Setting up a State Level Social Security Programme to integrate different programmes like health care, old-age pensions, emergency relief, price subsidies, food security and housing.
- Partnering with Unique Identification Authority (UIDAI) to integrate health, pension, conditional cash transfer to the people in the state.
- Setting up an Aid-Coordination Cell to integrate and channelise all aid flowing into the state like Central government aid, multilateral aid, international NGO aid etc.

Annexures

Annexure Table A-5

Financing

Key Factors	*Uttar Pradesh*	*India Best*	*India*
Per capita public expenditure	128	1082	n/a
Per capita private expenditure	846	170	n/a
Public expenditure as a percentage of total health care expenditure	13.10	71.7	n/a
Budegetary allocation 11th five year plan: 2007-2012 (Rs lakh)	1,319,405	1,319,405	n/a

Source: ORF Team Analysis.

Finance and Economic Data (Selective)

Annexure Table A-6

Trends in Total and Per Capita Income of India and Uttar Pradesh at Constant 1999-2000 Prices

	Net Income in Rs crore			*Per Capita Income in Rs*		
Year	*India*	*Uttar Pradesh*	*UP as % of India*	*India*	*Uttar Pradesh*	*Uttat Pradesh as % of India*
1999–2000	1585501	151283	9.5	15839	9405	59.38
2000–01	1643998	155564	9.5	16133	9451	58.58
2001–02	1739876	159613	9.2	16762	9475	56.53
2002–03	1801430	165647	9.2	17075	9657	56.56
2003–04*	1959599	174833	8.9	18263	9993	54.72
2004–05*$	2103350	182409	8.7	19297	10224	52.98
2005-06$	2295243	193457	8.4	20734	10637	51.3

Source: ORF Team Analysis.

Annexure Table A-7

Compound Annual Growth Rate (CAGR) of Total and Per Capita Income

Period	*CAGR of Total Income (%)*		*CAGR of Per Capita Income (%)*	
	Uttar Pradesh	*India*	*Uttar Pradesh*	*India*
1951-1956	2	3.6	0.5	1.7
1956-1961	1.9	4	0.3	1.9
1961-1966	1.6	2.2	-0.2	0
1966-1969	0.3	4	-1.5	1.8
1969-1974	2.3	3.3	0.4	1.1
1974-1979	5.7	5.3	3.3	2.9
1981-1985	8.7	5.3	6.3	3.1
1985-1990	5.7	5.8	3.3	3.6
1990-1992	3.1	2.5	1.1	0.4
1992-1997	3.2	6.8	1.4	4.9
1997-2002	2	5.6	-0.4	3.6
2002-2007	5.3	7.7	3.3	6

Source: ORF Team Analysis.

Annexure Table A-8

Finance: Uttar Pradesh

Year	*Real Growth Rate at Constant Prices*	*Public Debt (Outstanding Liabilities)*	*Revenue Deficit*	*Fiscal Deficit*	*Own Tax Revenue*	*Total Revenue Receipt*	*Public Debt (Total Liabilities)*	*Outlay on Roads & Bridges*	*Expenditure on Roads & Bridges*	*Value of Output from Mining & Quarrying at 1999-2000 Prices (All Minerals)*	*Employment in Organised Sector: Public*	*Employment in Organised Sector: Private*
	% GSDP							*Rs in lakh*			*Numbers in lakh*	
1999-2000	5.49	44.49	-4.14	-6.34	5.37	12.27	44.49			209344.0	20.3	5.2
2000-01	2.19	45.78	-3.46	-5.69	6.21	13.63	45.78			217135.0	17.6	4.7
2001-02	2.17	50.36	-3.36	-5.47	5.9	13.45	50.36			187227.0	17.2	4.6
2002-03	3.72	50.82	-2.7	-5.02	6.66	13.45	50.82			241675.0	16.5	4.4
2003-04	5.27	54.66	-8.19	-7.33	5.99	13.94	54.66			231679.0	16.4	4.5
2004-05	5.4	54.76	-2.81	-5.22	6.31	15.12	54.76			269667.0	16.5	4.4
2005-06	5.25	55.6	-0.46	-3.64	6.81	16.32	55.6			329292.0	16.4	4.6
2006-07	7.18	53.67	1.57	-3.08	7.36	19.38	53.67				16.3	4.83
2007-08	7.16	50.27	0.96	-3.86	6.98	19.21	50.27	392944	439535			
2008-09	6.46	47.92	1	-4.98	6.95	18.88	47.92	480495	522586			

Source: Planning Commission of India.

Annexure Table A-9

Finance and Energy Information: Uttar Pradesh

Year	Originally Approved Outlay	Revised Outlay	Actual Expnditure	Approved Outlay	Actual Expenditure	Below Poverty Line: URP	Electricity Available	Transmission & Distribution Loss	Total Energy Consumption
	Rs in crore			% of GSDP		(% of persons)	(GWH)	(%)	(GWH)
1999-2000	11400		6572.21	6.51	3.75	31.15			23469.4
2000-2001	9025		5956.4	4.97	3.28				25743.1
2001-2002	8400		5965.36	2.56	3.14				25230.2
2002-2003	7250		6618	3.5	3.2		38466.34	34.16	25184.4
2003-2004	7728		6132	3.4	2.7		41974.46	35.17	26659.6
2004-2005	9662		8428	3.88	3.39	32.8	42992.45	34.39	27939.3
2005-2006	13500		13522.85	4.87	4.88		45083.14	32.63	30374.2
2006-2007	19000	19000	20341.68	6.08	6.51		51937.13	33.49	34543.73
2007-2008	25000		24296.53	6.99	6.8		52568.34	28.6	37531.88
2008-2009	35000	32000.09	34287.62	8.49	8.32		57391.3	30.94	

Source: Planning Commission of India.

Infrastructure Data (Selective)

Annexure Table A-10

Power Supply Position

Year	Requirement	Availability	Surplus	Deficit	Peak Demand	Peak Met	Surplus	Deficit
	MU			%	MW			%
2009-10	75,930	59,508	-16,422	-21.6	10,856	8,563	-2,293	-21.1
2010-11	76,292	64,846	-11,446	-15	11,082	10,672	-410	-3.7

Source: ORF Team Analysis.

Annexure Table A-11

Road Data: Uttar Pradesh

Year	Total Length of Roads (km)	Surfaced Length of Roads (km)	Total Length of National Highways (km)	Surfaced Length of National Highways (km)	Total Length of State Highways (km)	Surfaced Length of State Highways (km)	Total PWD Roads (km)	Surfaced PWD Roads (km)
2004	244442	182057	5599	5599	9097	9097	113102	105980
2005	256683	168901	5599	5599	8888	8888	115109	108594
2006	263555	175151	5874	5874	8551	8551	118983	112986
2007	272362	185823	5874	5874	8449	8449	125252	119734
2008	284673	202492	5874	5874	8391	8391	138024	134516

Source: Basic Roads Statistics in India.

Participants in the Brainstorming Session Held on 26th August 2011 at ORF, New Delhi.

1. Surendra Singh, IAS (Former Cabinet Secretary, Honorary Advisor—ORF)
2. Satish Misra (Senior Fellow, ORF)
3. Saurabh Johri (Author of the paper)
4. D.P. Tripathi (General Secretary, Nationalist Congress Party)
5. S.C. Tripathi, IAS (Former Petroleum Secretary)
6. M. Ramachandran, IAS (Former Urban Development Ministry Secretary)
7. Ashok Rastogi, IAS (Secretary, Ministry of Home, Disaster Management)
8. Nirpendra Misra, IAS (Secretary Ministry of Communication)
9. Ashish Mitra, IPS (Former Special Secretary Internal Security, Ministry of Home, Former DG NSG)
10. Ajay Raj Sharma, IPS (Former Delhi Police Commissioner, former DG BSF)
11. Ajit K. Singh (Director, Giri Institute of Development, Lucknow)
12. Ravi S. Srivastava (Professor of Economics, Jawaharlal Nehru Universtiy)
13. Arvind Mohan (Professor of Economics, Lucknow University)
14. Brajendra N. Roy (Ex UN Advisor)
15. Rajni Khanna (The World Bank)
16. Sharat Pradhan (Uttar Pradesh based journalist)
17. Venkitesh Ramakrishna (Journalist, Frontline, working on Uttar Pradesh)
18. Yogesh Vajpayee (Journalist)
19. Shesh Narain Singh (Journalist)
20. Shishir Gupta (Economist)